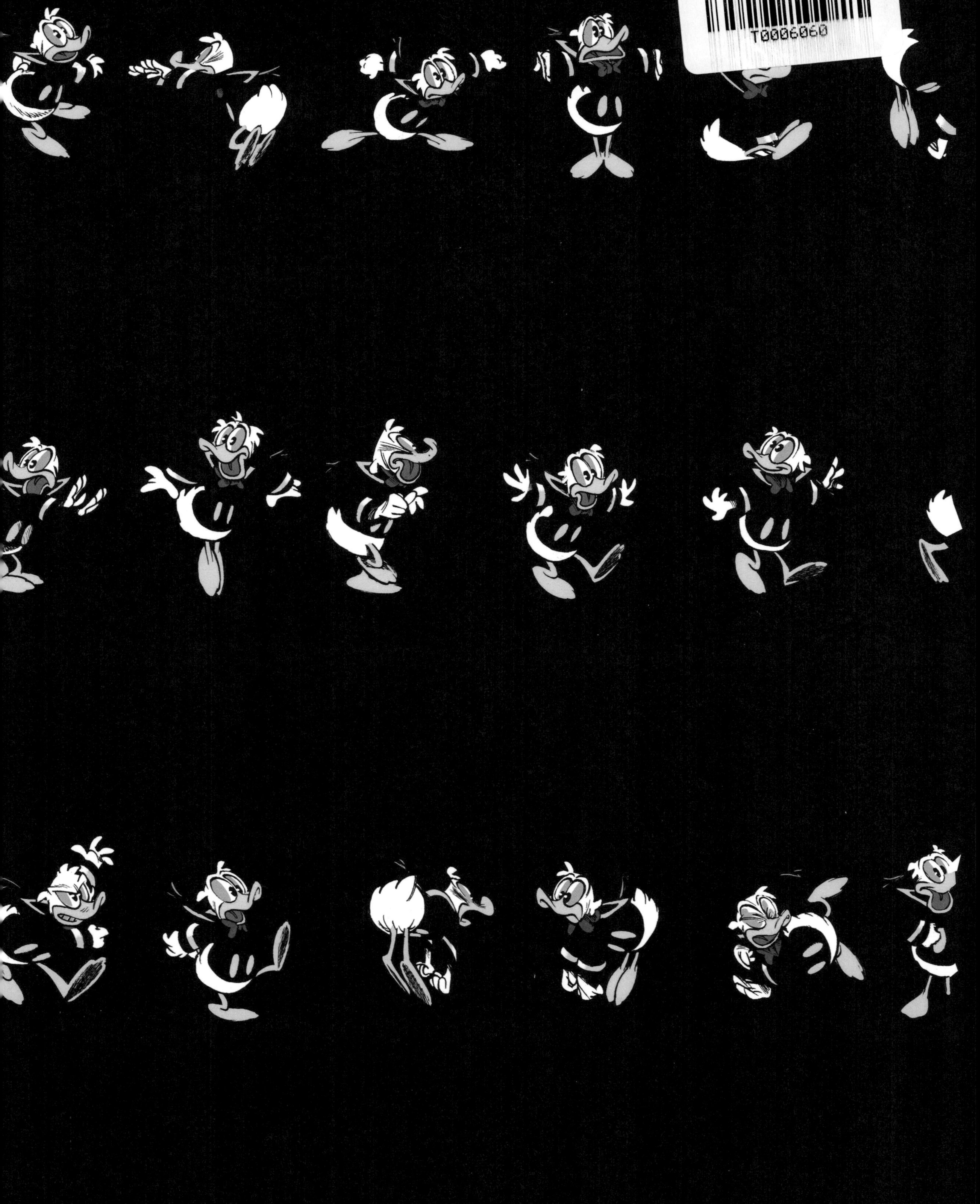

WALT DISNEY'S DONALD DUCK

DONALD'S
HAPPIEST ADVENTURES

Walt Disney Donald Duck

DONALD'S HAPPIEST ADVENTURES

STORY

LEWIS TRONDHEIM

ART

NICOLAS KERAMIDAS

COLOR

BRIGITTE FINDAKLY with
CHRISTINA HWANG

FANTAGRAPHICS
SEATTLE, WASHINGTON

Publisher: GARY GROTH
Editor: DAVID GERSTEIN
Translator: DAVID GERSTEIN
Designer: JUSTIN ALLAN-SPENCER and ÉDITIONS GLÉNAT
Lettering and Production: CHRISTINA HWANG
Associate Publisher: ERIC REYNOLDS

Fantagraphics Books, Inc.
7563 Lake City Way NE
Seattle WA 98115
(800) 657-1100

Visit us at fantagraphics.com
Follow us on Twitter at @fantagraphics
and on Facebook at facebook.com/fantagraphics.

First printing: January 2023
ISBN 978-1-68396-666-1
Printed in China

The feature story in this volume was first published in France,
and appears here in English for the first time.

FORTUNE NEVER COMES ALONE

BY ÉDITIONS GLÉNAT
INTRODUCTION TO THE 2018 FRENCH EDITION

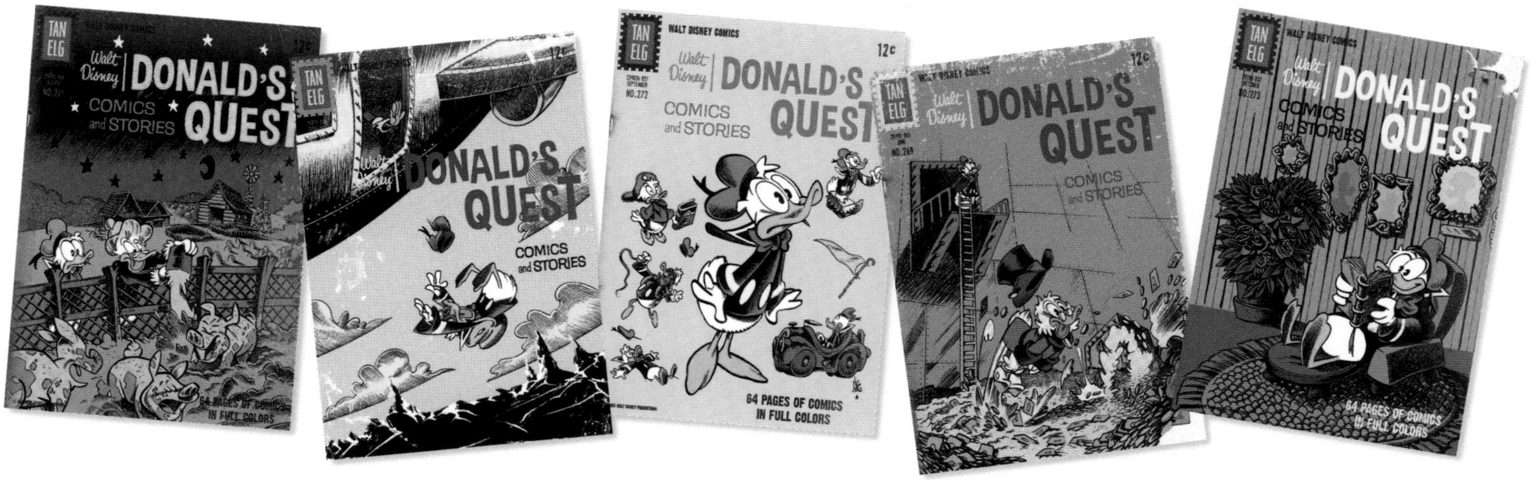
TAN ELG
Walt Disney
DONALD'S QUEST
COMICS and STORIES
12¢
64 PAGES OF COMICS IN FULL COLORS
WALT DISNEY COMICS

Several years ago at a garage sale, **Lewis Trondheim** and **Nicolas Keramidas** discovered some 40 issues of *Walt Disney's Comics and Stories: Mickey's Quest*, a rare spinoff comic book not archived at Disney and only ever distributed regionally. From this discovery was born *Mickey's Craziest Adventures*, a new edition of the same-named serial first published in those magazines.

On the strength of their garage sale find, Lewis and Nicolas did not take the road to retirement, but rather embarked on an even more in-depth historical excavation. Their *Mickey's Quest* discovery drove the pair further: not in pursuit of fame and fortune, but to salvage additional forgotten graphical and narrative treasures.

One day Lewis' and Nicolas' love of 1960s Disney comics pushed them past an antique-store tableful of Magic cards and steam irons. There it lay, quietly awaiting rediscovery: an extensive run of a later regional-only title, *Walt Disney's Comics and Stories: Donald's Quest*. But "extensive" was an understatement. Our two friends' eyes grew misty as they realized they held in their hands a *complete* set of this magazine. Unlike *Mickey's Quest* — where issues were missing, and therefore full pages of the "Mickey's Craziest Adventures" serial — Donald's *whole* serial, "Donald's Happiest Adventures," was there!

Sometimes the pages were a little torn, but this was nothing compared to Lewis' and Nicolas' own physical condition after a night's fiesta in celebration of this exciting discovery.

"Donald's Happiest Adventures" is fascinating not only for the beauty of its plotline and the humor scattered through its serialized pages, but also because it was — to the knowledge of our two authors — the only instance of a Disney comic story with serious philosophical significance. Indeed, Donald's search for happiness will delight both children and metaphysicians. Disney's cross-generational magic works!

As with *Mickey's Craziest*, Lewis translated the current story — full of twists and turns — into French for its modern Glénat publication, while Nicolas took up his pencils to provide a cover drawing that acts as a diptych with the first. To those naughty spirits who claim that we are inventing (yet again!) a cover story, and that *Mickey's Craziest* and *Donald's Happiest* are actually modern, newly-created serials, we reply that it is vital to preserve one's childlike sense of fun.

CHAPTER 1

BAD LUCK! *PHOOEY!*

BILLS AND MORE BILLS!

HEY, *JONES!* SAVE YOUR *WATER* FOR *BATHING,* STINKY!

HEY, *DUCK!* SAVE YOUR *DROOL* FOR LICKING *STAMPS!*

HI, UNCA DONALD!

BYE, UNCA DONALD!

WE BAKED A CAKE AND LEFT YOU A SLICE.

WHY, WHAT WELL-BEHAVED--

NO. I *WON'T* LOSE MY TEMPER. I'LL TOWEL OFF, GRAB A GOOD BOOK AND... *CHILL...*

KLONG

KLONG

KLONG

PLTCH!

YAAAH! TOO MUCH CHILL!

HERE WE GO AGAIN!

RRING

RRING RRING

NEPHEW! GET YOUR TAIL HERE *TOOT SWEET!*

I'VE GOT AN *URGENT* AND *DANGEROUS* JOB FOR YOU.

HMPH.

I WAS SO *HAPPY* TILL HE CALLED.

BEEP BEEP!

AW, PIPE DOWN! YA BIG...

MICKEY!

DONALD!

GIMME A RIDE TO UNCLE SCROOGE'S -- *QUICK!*

AGAIN?

SMOLEY HOKES, *NO!* I REMEMBER WHAT HAPPENED *LAST* TIME! FER GOSH *SAKES!*

HEY!

TWENTY DOL- LARS.

THAT'S MY *SEVENTH* TWENTY-DOLLAR BILL TODAY. C'MON, NOT A *SINGLE* OCEAN CRUISE TICKET? I'M REALLY FEELING *UNLUCKY* HERE!

?!

CRACK!

SPLUG!

OBOY! THIS DISGUSTING WASTE WATER IS CARRYING ME *DOWNTOWN* -- RIGHT NEAR UNCLE SCROOGE'S MONEY BIN!

FINALLY SOME *LUCK!*

UNCLE SCROOGE, CAN I USE YOUR *SHOWER*?

GROWF!

THAT'LL BE *$3* FOR *WATER*!

Get Out!

SCRAM!

hie thee hence!

~GURGLE!~ *HALP!* I CAN'T MAKE IT GO *HOT!*

I DON'T *PAY* FOR HOT.

YOU WANT ME TO GO *BROKE*?

SHEESH! INSTALL A *SOLAR-POWERED* WATER HEATER, AND YOU CAN HAVE HOT WATER FOR *FREE*.

BAM!

YOU *TRAITOR!*

TAKE THAT *BACK!* YOU TAKE THAT BACK RIGHT NOW!

HUH?

TAKE BACK "BAM"?

NOT THAT! THE THING YOU SAID ABOUT SOLAR POWER, SILLY!

HOW DO YOU THINK I *MADE* MY FORTUNE? ~SNORT!~ INVESTING IN *COAL, GAS, OIL...* FOSSIL FUELS!

IF I INSTALLED A *SOLAR* WATER HEATER, WHAT KIND OF *EXAMPLE* WOULD THAT SET?

OTHERS WOULD GO SOLAR *TOO* -- AND MY *BUSINESSES* WOULD GO *BUST!*

SO INVEST IN SOLAR! YOU'D STAY ON TOP *AND* GIVE PEOPLE HEALTHIER AIR TO BREATHE!

IMPOSSIBLE!

I NEED PEOPLE *SICK!* I OWN TEN COUGH DROP FACTORIES!

WHATEVER, UNCLE SCROOGE. I'M *READY.*

EXPLAIN MY URGENT, DANGEROUS JOB.

RIGHT! DEEP IN THE VIRGIN FORESTS OF CHILIBURGERIA, I'VE HEARD TELL OF A *BURIED TREASURE!*

HIDDEN IN A *FORGOTTEN* AZTEC TEMPLE! GUARDED BY TERRIBLE *TRAPS...*

JAR AFTER JAR OF *PRICELESS* GOLD COINS!

I'VE GOT A HALF-LEGIBLE OLD SCROLL TO SHOW YOU THE WAY!

PFFT.

ANOTHER DEADLY TREASURE TEMPLE. AROUND HERE WE CALL THAT "TUESDAY."

LOOK, UNK! WHY *ME?* WHY MUST *I* SCOUR THE GLOBE FOR THESE UNFINDABLE HOARDS?

BECAUSE *I'M* TOO *OLD* TO DO IT *ALL!*

BUT WILL WE EVER *STOP?*

WHY DO YOU NEED *NEW* FERSHLUGGINER TREASURES ALL THE TIME? YOU'RE RICH *ENOUGH.*

NONSENSE! FILLING MY BIN FILLS *ME* WITH JOY...

...AND I'M *NOT* AS JOYFUL AS I COULD BE! I *KNOW* IT!

SO YOU AREN'T LOOKING FOR *LOOT,* UNCLE SCROOGE. YOU'RE LOOKING FOR *TRUE HAPPINESS.*

WOWSY! THAT *WOULD* BE A TREASURE.

NEPHEW, YOU'RE ONTO SOMETHING! FIND ME THE *SECRET* OF *HAPPINESS!*

G'WAN! *GIT!*

UH-OH! THOSE AZTEC COINS WOULDA BEEN A THOUSAND TIMES EASIER!

HOW DOES ONE EVEN *START* LOOKING FOR THE SECRET OF *HAPPINESS?* —¡GRUNT!—

?!

HEY!

TWENTY DOLLARS. MEH.

OHO! I KNOW!

I'LL SPY ON MY *ENDLESSLY LUCKY* COUSIN GLADSTONE!

...AND *ANOTHER* TWENTY DOLLARS.

GLORY BE! WHAT DO I SEE?

BAH! YET *ANOTHER* TWENTY DOLLARS!

C'MON!

IT *CAN'T* BE!

...ANOTHER TWENTY DOLLARS...

OHO! THERE WE GO! AN *OCEAN CRUISE* TICKET!

FEH!

A *SECOND-CLASS* OCEAN CRUISE TICKET. *NEXT*, PLEASE.

GAD! THAT *IS* LUCK.

...HE'S *LITTERED* ON THE PAVEMENT *THREE* TIMES, WITHOUT A COP COMING OVER TO FINE HIM *ONCE!*

AWRIGHT, CONNOISSEUR OF THE FAST BUCK! HOW WOULD YOU DEFINE *HAPPINESS*?

?!

HA! EASY! FINDING A *FIRST-CLASS* OCEAN CRUISE TICKET!

OHO!

A. CRUISE WOULD MAKE YOU *HAPPY*.

YAHS!

UNTIL...

...I CAME *HOME* FROM IT. -*PFT!*-

AND THEN YOU'D BE *SAD*?

TILL I FOUND A COUPON FOR A FREE *BACK MASSAGE* -- NATURALLY!

AFTER DAYS SPRAWLED ON A DECKCHAIR, DOZING AGAIN AND AGAIN, A PERSON CAN DEVELOP A *PAIN*.

I *SEE*. SO A *MASSAGE* WILL MAKE YOU HAPPY?

NO WAY, CUZ! NOT TILL I *ALSO* FIND A COUPON FOR A *FREE GOURMET DINNER* AT THE *PLATINUM PAN!*

AND A NIGHT AT *ANY* FIVE-STAR HOTEL.

OH! AND THE NEXT DAY, I'D NEED TO FIND *ANOTHER* CRUISE TICKET. I CAN *NEVER* DIGEST BIG DINNERS WITHOUT BRISK SEA AIR TO HELP ME.

LIFE ISN'T FAIR.

HEY!... AW, NUTBUNNIES. A WHOLE *WALLETFUL* OF TWENTIES AND *NO* FIRST-CLASS CRUISE TICKET.

I KNOW WHO COULD HELP ME -- SOMEONE WHO *REALLY* LEADS A *HAPPY LIFE.*

QUACK TOWN
POP. 439
"PEACEFULNESS PLUS"

HI-DE-HI, GRANDMA! HI, COUSIN GUS!

HOWDY, DONALD!

WHAT ILL WIND BLOWS *YOU* IN?

-:GROAN!:- UNCLE SCROOGE ASKED ME TO FIND THE SECRET OF TRUE HAPPINESS! I, UH... SORTA FIGURED YOU KNEW IT!

WHAT.

'FRAID I AIN'T GOT A *CLUE,* GRANDSON!

BUT YOU'RE *HAPPY,* RIGHT?

'COURSE I AM.

BUT YOU THINK *SCROOGE* WOULD BE HAPPY, SLOPPIN' HOGS AN' MILKIN' COWS?

NO, ACTUALLY...

SEE -- TH' NOTION OF HAPPINESS IS *DIFFERENT* FOR *DIFFERENT* FOLKS!

SO HOW WOULD *I* FIND IT?

BY *FORGETTIN' SCROOGE* FOR FIVE MINUTES.

NOT GONNA HAPPEN.

NOPE. NIX. POOH.

WANNA *BET,* SONNY?

SUCCULENT BLUEBERRY PIE. GREAT STUFF! GREAT STUFF!

HI, GUS!

HI, UNCA DONALD!

HI, GRANDMA!

DON'T MIND US! JUST RESEARCHING CLINTON COOT'S OLD FAMILY PAPERS...

NO MAKING A *MESS!* SAVVY?

AN' WHAT ARE YOU BOYS *LOOKING* FOR IN MY FATHER'S PAPERS?

HIS *ORIGINAL MANUSCRIPT* FOR THE *JUNIOR WOODCHUCK GUIDEBOOK,* GRANDMA.

SEE -- WE THINK HE INCLUDED *RARE FACTS* THAT DIDN'T MAKE IT INTO THE *PUBLISHED* VERSION OF THE GUIDE!

->SNORT!<- A *MESS* ALREADY! I *KNEW* IT!

SLOW DOWN, YOU BRATNIKS!

CAN'T!

THIS IS *IMPORTANT!*

IT'S OUR *TICKET* TO FINDING ALL THE SECRETS IN THE WORLD!

HEY!... *I'M* LOOKING FOR A *SECRET!*

BUT GRANDMA DUCK, YORE *GOAT* AIN'T BATHED IN *WEEKS!* YUH REALLY WANT ME TA BRING HIM IN HERE?

YEP! DONALD AN' TH' BOYS WON'T *LEAVE* TILL HE BUTTS THEM *OUT!*

GOT IT! THE MANUSCRIPT!

EEK!

PAK

?!

MOO-HOO!

GOTTA CATCH UP!

SHE'S RUNNING TOO FAST!

PUFF!

PUFF!

PUFF!

OUT OF SIGHT!

-SIGH!- JUST OUR BAD LUCK!

I WAS SO HAPPY, KNOWING THE SECRET OF HAPPINESS WAS NEAR!

IF YOU WERE HAPPY ALREADY, WHY DO YOU NEED THE SECRET OF HAPPINESS?

OH, I SEE HOW IT IS! LEAVE ME CONFUSED WHILE YOU GO FINISH THE BLUEBERRY PIE!

MIGHTY GOOD OF YOU TO BAKE AN EXTRA PIE JUST FOR ME!

MY PLEASURE, DONALD.

IT CREATES MORE *HAPPINESS* TO GIVE THAN TO RECEIVE.

EH?

RECEIVING IS A *SELFISH* PLEASURE...

...WHILE *GIVING* BRINGS TH' *DEEPER* SATISFACTION OF *SHARING LOVE.*

I'LL BE DOGGONED!... THANKS, GRANDMA. BUT I'LL NEVER SELL *UNCLE SCROOGE* ON HAPPINESS THROUGH *GIVING.*

HEH! OLD SCROOGE WOULDN'T *GIVE* A MAN THE TIME WITH HIS POCKETWATCH IN HIS HAND!

HE'D NEVER GIVE LESSONS!

HE'D NEVER GIVE HANDSHAKES!

TEE HEE!

~HAW!~ HE CAN'T EVEN GIVE *DIRECTIONS!*

HEY, GRANDMA DUCK! UNCLE SCROOGE ON TH' PHONE.

DONALD! I HEARD YOU MOCKING ME! HIDING WILL GET YOU NOWHERE! I'M GONNA *GIVE* YOU A *TALKING-TO...*

ER... I MEAN. YOU WILL *RECEIVE* A TALKING-TO.

DONALD...

...A *GUEST* IS HERE TO SEE YOU.

UNCLE *SCROOGE?*

WHOA, MULE! *NO.* I ASKED YOUR UNCLE *LUDWIG* TO CALL.

BEIN' AN *EXPERT* ON *EVERYTHING,* HE'LL *SURELY* HELP YOU ON THIS HAPPINESS HUNT!

HOWDY!

HALLO!

EXCUSE ME!

TAH-DAH!

YOO-HOO! IT'S ME!.

WHERE'S THE *CONFERENCE* YOU INVITED THE GREAT VON DRAKE TO, HUH?

UH... YOU'RE JUST HERE FOR DONALD...

FINE! NO BIG! NEXT TOPIC!

THIS *SAPPY NEST* THINGIE! IS THE *SAPPY BIRD* AT HOME?

MY *ORNITHOLOGY DEGREE* IS *ALL READY* FOR YOU!

I SAID *HAPPINESS.* NOT *SAPPY NEST.*

HMM...

TOO BAD.

I BROUGHT 600 POUNDS OF *IRON-ZINC BIRDSEED* TO MAKE SAPPY BIRDS TOUGHER! NOW I WON'T NEED IT!

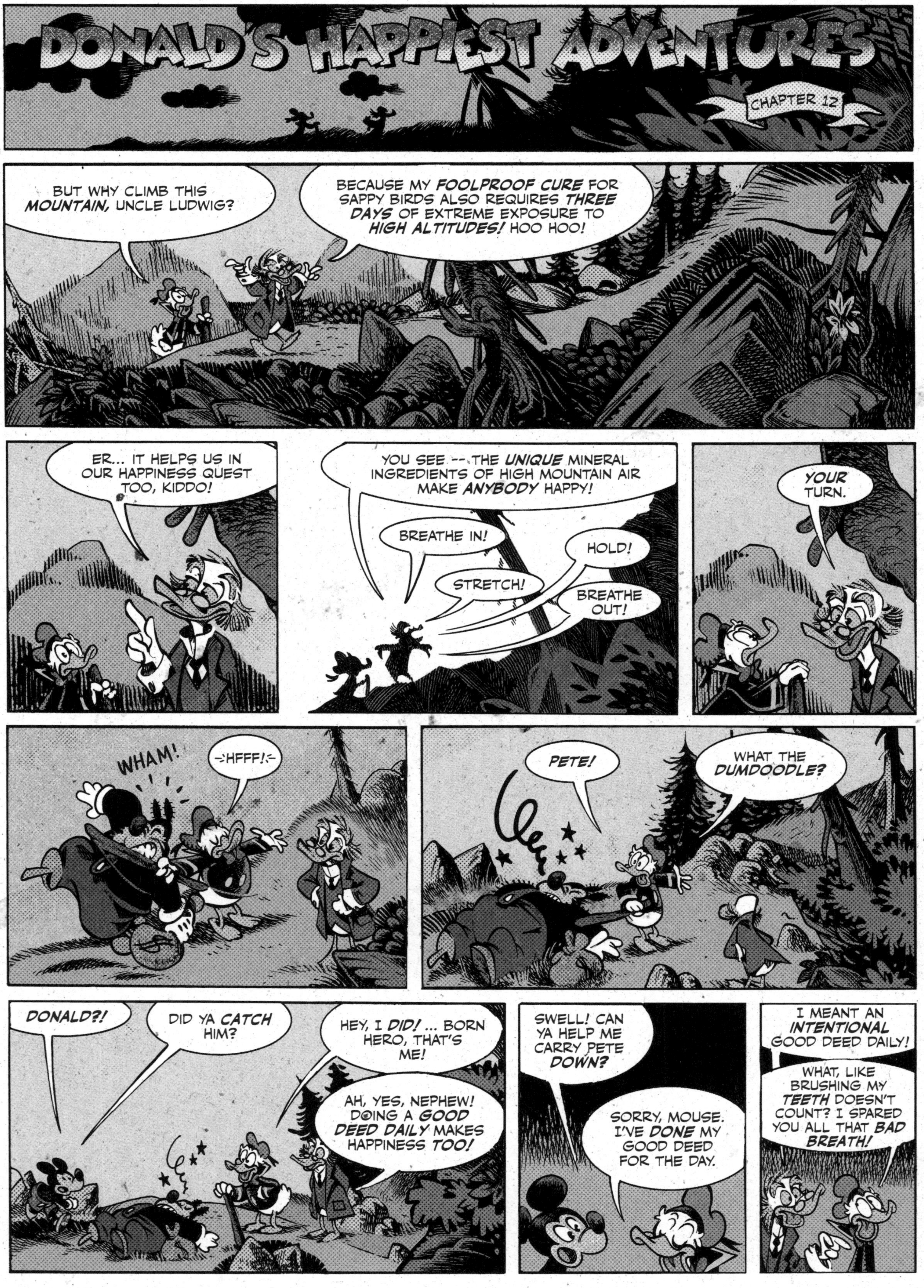
DONALD'S HAPPIEST ADVENTURES
CHAPTER 12
BUT WHY CLIMB THIS MOUNTAIN, UNCLE LUDWIG?
BECAUSE MY FOOLPROOF CURE FOR SAPPY BIRDS ALSO REQUIRES THREE DAYS OF EXTREME EXPOSURE TO HIGH ALTITUDES! HOO HOO!
ER... IT HELPS US IN OUR HAPPINESS QUEST TOO, KIDDO!
YOU SEE -- THE UNIQUE MINERAL INGREDIENTS OF HIGH MOUNTAIN AIR MAKE ANYBODY HAPPY!
BREATHE IN!
STRETCH!
HOLD!
BREATHE OUT!
YOUR TURN.
WHAM!
-HFFF!-
PETE!
WHAT THE DUMDOODLE?
DONALD?!
DID YA CATCH HIM?
HEY, I DID! ... BORN HERO, THAT'S ME!
AH, YES, NEPHEW! DOING A GOOD DEED DAILY MAKES HAPPINESS TOO!
SWELL! CAN YA HELP ME CARRY PETE DOWN?
SORRY, MOUSE. I'VE DONE MY GOOD DEED FOR THE DAY.
I MEANT AN INTENTIONAL GOOD DEED DAILY!
WHAT, LIKE BRUSHING MY TEETH DOESN'T COUNT? I SPARED YOU ALL THAT BAD BREATH!

MICKEY TOLD ME YE CAUGHT PETE, LAD...

AND CARRIED HIM DOWN! I *ALMOST* DIDN'T NEED TO BE COAXED.

FAITH AN' BEJABBERS, *FINE.* HERE'S YOUR *CASH REWARD*...

AND A HEARTY *THANKS.*

?!

SO, DONNY BOY! IS HAPPINESS BROUGHT TO HEEL? (WE'LL TEACH IT TO PLAY FETCH NEXT!)

YES!

PIZZA PARTY!

MASSAGE MASSACRE!

CRUISE CONTROL!

REPEAT-ZA PARTY!

AW, PHOOEY! I'M FLAT-BUSTED *BROKE!*

AND THE *MORAL* OF THIS KOOKY STORY *IS...*

UH...

NEXT TIME I *HELP PETE ESCAPE* SO I CAN *RECAPTURE* HIM FOR A *SECOND* REWARD! YES? NO?

DONALD'S HAPPIEST ADVENTURES

CHAPTER 14

POOH! YOU'VE LEARNED A BIG FAT *NOTHING*, NEPHEW. I AM VAMOOSING! MUSH! MUSH!

NO! NO! NO!

I *NEED* YOU!

YOU NEED ME *BECAUSE* I AM AN AMAZING FOUNT OF KNOWLEDGE... AND YOU ARE A SAPPY BIRD!

NO! *BECAUSE* IF I DON'T FIND THE SECRET OF HAPPINESS, UNCLE SCROOGE WILL *TAR* AND *PLUCK* ME!

SORRY, KIDDO! SCAREDY CATS DON'T FIND SECRETS!

JUST WEAR A SKINDIVING SUIT! THEN THE TAR CAN'T TOUCH YOU!

I GOTTA *JET* FOR A SCIENCE CONFERENCE IN *BRUTOPIA*, ANYWAY!

BRUTOPIA!... ISN'T THAT COUNTRY RULED BY AN *AWFUL TYRANT?*

THE PEOPLE THERE ARE ALL *VERY UNHAPPY!*

NO. NOT *ALL.*

THERE IS *ONE* BRUTOPIAN WHO IS *VERY* HAPPY.

SWELL! I'D LOVE TO MEET HIM!

GREETINGS, PROFESSOR LUDWIG VON DRAKE!

HERE HE IS NOW.

MY COUNTRY, BRUTOPIA, IS *THRILLED* TO RECEIVE YOU, WISE OWL OF A DUCK!

TAKE A SEAT ON THE PLANE, PLEASE.

HOW CAN HE BE *VERY HAPPY* IN *BRUTOPIA?!*

HE'S THEIR *PRESIDENT...* THE TYRANT, HIMSELF!

DONALD'S HAPPIEST ADVENTURES

CHAPTER 15

WE LAND IN THREE HOURS. WOULD YOU LIKE A *SNACK* TO PASS THE TIME, WISE OWL OF A DUCK?

WE HAVE SPAGHETTI SANDWICH PIES, PUREED LASAGNA SOUFFLÉS...

...AND RATATOUILLE FRENCH-FRY SOUP...

HOLD THE PHONE! WHY IS EVERY DISH *THREE-IN-ONE*?

HEH! HEH!

BECAUSE BRUTOPIA'S HAPPY PEOPLE HAVE VERY LITTLE TO *EAT!* I GET EXTRA *PLEASURE* GULPING DOWN THREE MEALS AT A TIME!

SO WHY STOP THERE? WHY DON'T YOU SCRAMBLE *NINE* ENTREES TOGETHER?

EGAD! NINE ENTREES! GOOD PLAN!

YOU OUGHT TO BECOME MY NEW *MINISTER OF IDEAS!*

UNLESS HE'S AN *ENEMY SPY* TRYING TO *STUFF* YOU TILL YOU'RE *SICK,* SIR!

...BUT I HADN'T SAID A *WORD* TO THAT HAIRY COYOTE! WHY'D HE PICK ON *ME?*

HE'S THE *OLD* MINISTER OF IDEAS!

HIP HIP HOORAY, DONALD! THAT WAS *WUNDERBAR*, WATCHING YOU GULP DOWN NINE DISHES AT ONCE -- JUST TO *PROVE* YOU MEANT *NO HARM* TO THE PRESIDENT OF BRUTOPIA!

MEH. I WAS HUNGRY.

SO, MR. PRESIDENT! *WHEN* WILL MY SCIENCE CONFERENCE START... AND *HOW LONG* WILL IT RUN? HO, HO!

IT WILL *START* WHEN YOU GO *BACK* BEHIND BARS -- AND IT WILL CONTINUE FOR *THIRTY YEARS.*

MY COUNTRY, BRUTOPIA, HAS SUFFERED A TERRIBLE BRAIN DRAIN! *YOU*, WISE OWL OF A DUCK, WILL FILL OUR KNOWLEDGE GAP.

SO YOU'RE *DUCKNAPPING* US! WHY, YOU... YOU *AWFUL TYRANT*, YOU!

YES! USING YOUR BRAINPOWER, BRUTOPIA WILL BUILD UP ITS *ARMY* AND *TECH SUPPLY* TO *EARTH-CONQUERING* SIZE!

SOON, I WILL NOT ONLY BE THE HAPPIEST OF *BRUTOPIA'S* HAPPY PEOPLE...

...BUT THE HAPPIEST ON THE *PLANET!*

HMM! MY PSYCHOLOGY DEGREE SAYS YOU'RE DOING THIS 'CAUSE NOBODY EVER *LIKED* YOU. PUT ON A CUTE *BAMBI* MASK. PEOPLE WILL *LOVE* YOU *THEN!*

SEE? *CHEAPER* SOLUTION.

DOGGONE! HE HAS A JAIL CELL IN HIS *CAR*, TOO.

DONALD'S HAPPIEST ADVENTURES

CHAPTER 17

DIG THAT SMOKE, UNCLE LUDWIG! THIS IS ONE *UGLY* COUNTRY.

DO NOT SPEAK THE *TRUTH!* YOU MUST *CHEER* FOR BRUTOPIA!

YES, WE LACK FOR EVERYTHING... FACTORIES, STEEL, ENGINEERS...

BUT WHAT *OTHER COUNTRIES* DO NOT *LOAN* US, WE WILL *TAKE BY FORCE!*

THAT BIG GOOFUS IS RIGHT! THESE CHAINS AREN'T STEEL!

NOPE! JUST PAINTED CARDBOARD!

ACH!

AND THIS *WINDOW* ISN'T *GLASS!* JUST *PLASTIC!*

WE CAN ESCAPE EASY! OH, BROTHER!

WE GIVE UP! THREE CHEERS FOR BRUTOPIA!

HA! THAT'S BETTER!

IT EVEN SOUNDED *SINCERE.*

I'M STARVING! I'M *PARCHED!* MY FEET ARE KILLING ME!

WE'LL DEAL WITH ALL THAT AFTER WE ACHIEVE *GOAL NUMBER ONE...* *LEAVING* BRUTOPIA!

WAK!

A *HOUSE!*

OBOY! OBOY! WE CAN CALL DUCKBURG AND GET SOME HELP!

FAT CHANCE! THE POOR FELLAS LIVING HERE DON'T HAVE *ELECTRICITY* FOR *PHONES,* KIDDO!

?

NO RUNNING WATER, EITHER! TSK, TSK!

NO CENTRAL HEATING...

NO WINDOWS...

NO *DOORS!*

YEAH!

THIS IS MEGA NUTS!

CAN YOU *IMAGINE?*

THEY DON'T EVEN HAVE *TV!*

HO, HO! THIS CHARACTER'S GOTTA BE THE OWNER!

~HYEE-HEE!~ NO, NO. I AM NOT THE OWNER OF THIS MANSION.

EVERYTHING I *OWN* IS WITH ME IN MY *HANDBAG*. SEE?

WHAT'S IN THERE? CANDY BARS?

A DICTIONARY?

NO. A *BIG ROCK*.

I USE IT AS A PILLOW.

IT'S NOT EXACTLY... UH, *COMFY*...

BUT IF I *LOSE* IT, OR IT IS *STOLEN*, I WON'T BE UNHAPPY! I HAVE MANY *MORE* BIG ROCKS AVAILABLE!

YOU WON'T BE... UH... SO YOU'RE *HAPPY* NOW?

TOTALLY.

I HAVE NO POSSESSIONS TO LOSE -- NOR ANY DESIRE FOR GAIN!

THE DIRT GIVES ME TASTY ROOTS TO MUNCH... AND THE SKY IS MY CEILING... WITH THIS *BEAUTIFUL VIEW*!

VIEW! WAIT A SEC!... ARE YOU SAYING WE'RE ON *CAMERA?* AND IF WE'RE SEEN *COMPLAINING* ABOUT BRUTOPIA, WE'LL GO TO *JAIL?*

LA-LA-LAH! I DIDN'T SAY THAT! YOU HEAR?

EGAD! DO YOU *REALLY* THINK WE'RE BEING *FILMED* AND SUCHLIKE?

IF WE ARE, I WILL *THANK* OUR *BELOVED PRESIDENT!*

PFAH! HE MAKES YOU BELIEVE IT, BUT WHERE'S THE *EVIDENCE?* POOH!

BESIDES, MR. PREZ DOESN'T HAVE THE *BUCKS* TO BUY ALL THE *CAMERAS* IT WOULD TAKE...

AND IF HE *HAD* THEM, HE'D HAVE *FOUND* US FUGITIVES BY NOW!

DARN TOOTIN'!

FUGITIVES?!

THE FUGITIVES ARE HERE!

THE FUGITIVES ARE HERE!

THE FUGITIVES ARE HERE!

LET'S CATCH A *NAP*, DONNY BOY!

THE FUGITIVES ARE HERE!

ZZ!

ZZ!

THE FUGITIVES ARE HERE!

I SLEPT GREAT! AND *YOU*, NEPHEW?

MM?

⇒SNORT!⇐ I THINK THE A/C WAS SET TOO LOW.

I'M COLD.

SO, YOKEL! HOW DOES IT *FEEL* TO FIND OUT YOU ARE *FREE* TO SPEAK AS YOU WISH, EH?

IS THAT NOT A LITTLE HAPPINESS?

NO! NO! THEY'RE *WATCHING* US! THEY'LL THROW US IN *JAIL*, BY CRACKY!

HMF! HE'S THE CRACKY ONE!

FOR *HIM* TO BE HAPPY, HE'S GOTTA BE SURE THE *WORST* WILL HAPPEN! AND THEN IF IT DOESN'T HAPPEN, HE'S HAPPY!

WE'LL BE FORCED TO LICK OUR CELL FLOORS FOR SUSTENANCE!

YOU'VE CURED HIM WITH YOUR DEGREE IN HYPNOSIS?

JA! HYPNOSIS IS AN *INFALLIBLE* SCIENCE... JUST LIKE NUCLEAR PHYSICS!

YOU MUST *COME OUT OF YOUR SHELL*, YOKEL! *THAT* IS YOUR JAIL! *STOP* BEING AFRAID...

...AND START SAYING WHAT YOU *REALLY THINK*, EH? *THEN* YOU WILL BE *FREE*!

IS THAT ALL?

HO, HO! WELL... NORMALLY, I WOULD FINISH BY *BILLING* MY PATIENT... OR IF I'M AT A CONFERENCE, BY GETTING APPLAUSE...

YOU ARE *BADLY DRESSED*.

?

ARE *THOSE* CLOTHES ALL THEY'VE GOT IN YOUR COUNTRY'S STORES?

SUCCESS! HE'S SAYING WHAT HE THINKS!

LET'S GO! I WANNA *SEE* YOUR COUNTRY... RUN AWAY FROM BRUTOPIA...

STAY THIRTY FEET BEHIND ME, GUYS! YOU DON'T SMELL GOOD, EITHER!

HEY!... AND *YOU* DON'T GOTTA BE SUCH A KOOKY *COMPLAINER*, BUSTER!

SHUT YOUR MOUTH, PLEASE! I'D PREFER THAT.

COULD YOU *UN-HYPNOTIZE* HIM, UNCLE LUDWIG?

IF HE STARTS TALKING ABOUT MY RECEDING HAIRLINE... YOU *BETCHA*!

LOOK!

IF YOU'RE HUNGRY, PICK UP A BIG FLAT ROCK...

...AND MAKE YOURSELF A PLATE!

AND TO EAT?

JUST LET NATURE PROVIDE!

SEE?

ROOTS!

GO AHEAD! GORGE WITHOUT GUILT!

IT TAKES *SKILL* TO BE AS HAPPY WITH A *ROOT* AS WITH A *ROYAL FEAST!*

⇥GLEEP!⇤ NEEDS MORE SALT... KETCHUP, MUSTARD, TOMATOES, PICKLES, AND FRENCH FRIES!

I *GUESS* THIS QUALIFIES AS LIVING OFF THE LAND!

BUT HAVE YOU GOT *WATER?*

YES! AND TODAY WE WON'T EVEN HAVE TO *DIG* FOR IT!

AT LAST SOME *GOOD NEWS* HERE AT DYSFUNCTION JUNCTION!

RUMBLE RUMBLE GUZZLE

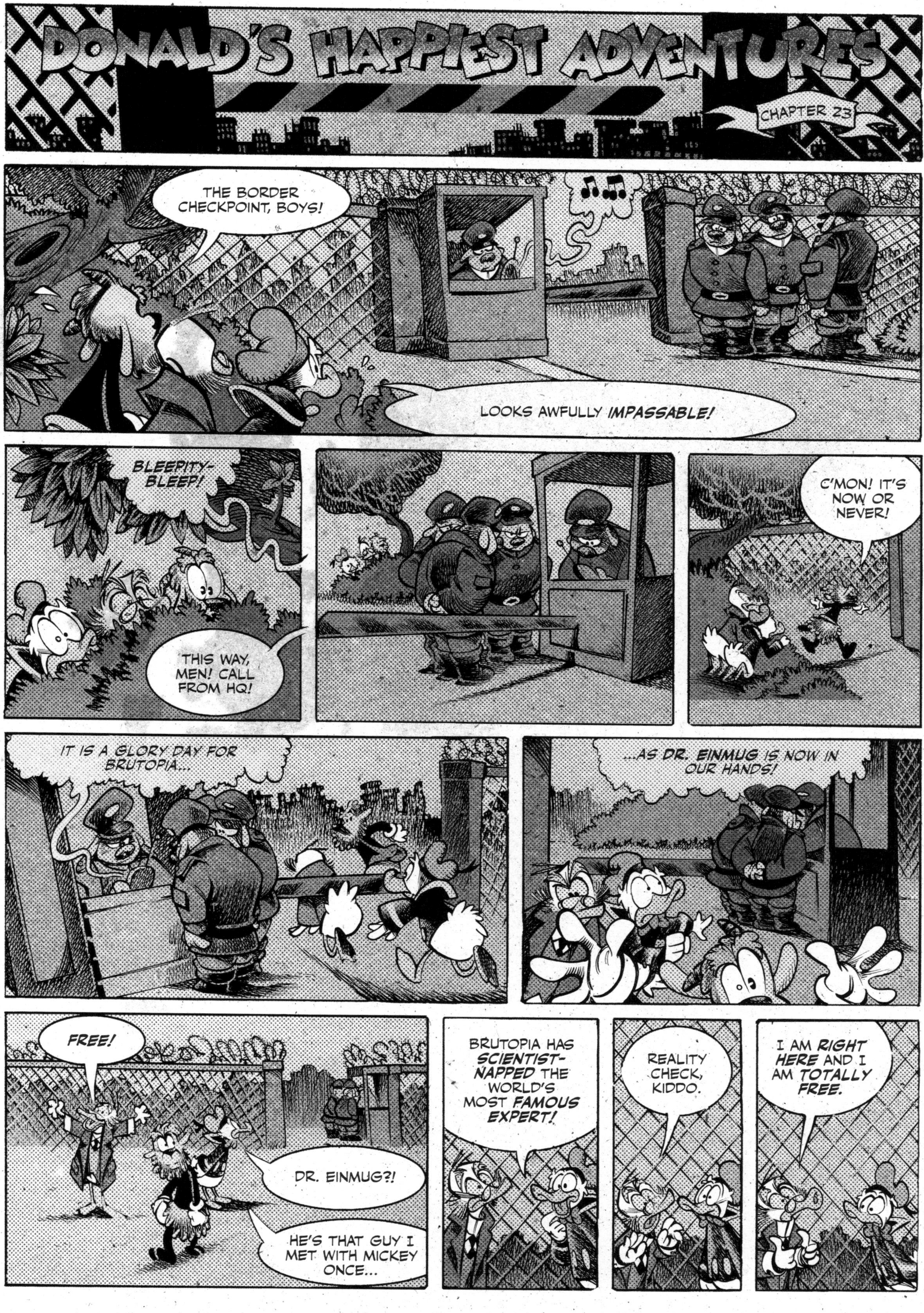
DONALD'S HAPPIEST ADVENTURES
CHAPTER 23
THE BORDER CHECKPOINT, BOYS!
LOOKS AWFULLY *IMPASSABLE!*
BLEEPITY-BLEEP!
THIS WAY, MEN! CALL FROM HQ!
C'MON! IT'S NOW OR NEVER!
IT IS A GLORY DAY FOR BRUTOPIA...
...AS DR. EINMUG IS NOW IN OUR HANDS!
FREE!
DR. EINMUG?!
HE'S THAT GUY I MET WITH MICKEY ONCE...
BRUTOPIA HAS *SCIENTIST-NAPPED* THE WORLD'S MOST *FAMOUS EXPERT!*
REALITY CHECK, KIDDO.
I AM *RIGHT HERE* AND I AM *TOTALLY FREE.*

WE'VE GOTTA *REENTER* BRUTOPIA AND GET DR. EINMUG *OUT!*

HIS BRAIN IS *GINORMOUS!* AND IN THE WRONG HANDS... WELL, ANYTHING'S POSSIBLE!

COUNT ME OUT! I'D RATHER GO VISIT YOUR CAPITALIST COUNTRY!

COUNT *ME* OUT, TOO! I CAN'T HAVE THOSE BRUTOPI-FELLAS STEALING *MY* BRAIN AGAIN!

-:GROAN!:- I DON'T ASK FOR MUCH! BUT HOW CAN I EXPECT TO BE *HAPPY,* WITH SOME *BIG-CHEEKBONED TYRANT RULER* THREATENING CLUCKS WHO I CARE ABOUT?

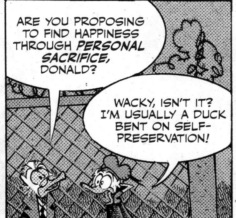

ARE YOU PROPOSING TO FIND HAPPINESS THROUGH *PERSONAL SACRIFICE,* DONALD?

WACKY, ISN'T IT? I'M USUALLY A DUCK BENT ON SELF-PRESERVATION!

-:HMM!:- VER-R-RY INTERESTING! LET'S REMEMBER THIS NEXT TIME WE TALK TO SCROOGE!

SO YOU CAN BOTH *LAUGH* AT ME?

NO WAY, NEPHEW!

IN FACT, WE CAN CALL HIM NOW! COME, COME!

HE'LL BE *HAPPY* TO PROTECT HIS FINANCIAL EMPIRE FROM A LOOMING CONFLICT!

EH?

WHAT?

BRUTOPIA'S CAPTURED A *FAMOUS EGGHEAD?*

SO? IS *INTERNATIONAL MEDIATION* ON ITS WAY?

ER... SCROOGE THANKED ME FOR MY CALL...

...AND TOLD ME HE'D BE INVESTING IN SURVIVAL SHELTERS.

DR. EINMUG...

YOU WILL BE *HAPPY* TO KNOW BRUTOPIA HAS *RECAPTURED* YOUR *COLLEAGUE* PROFESSOR VON DRAKE!

HIMMEL!

WE LOOK FORWARD TO USING *ALL* OF YOUR KNOWLEDGE!

BOOMF

?

YOU ARE NOT--

IX-NAY!

IT'S ME, DONALD DUCK! MICKEY AND I VISITED YOUR LAB IN THE DESERT, AND WE TRAVELLED TO THE EARTH'S CORE... WITH DINOSAURS...

IT DOESN'T RING A BELL!

A *GIANT METEOR* FELL ON US!

I CANNOT RECALL!

WE RODE ON THIS *PTERODACTYL* TO ESCAPE FROM A T-REX WITH FEATHERS!

ACH, YAH?

⌐SIGH⌐ I TRIPPED ON MAMMOTH POOP.

UFF COURSE!

DONALD!

DO YOU HAFF A PLAN TO *ESCAPE* FROM HERE?

MINE BRAINPOWER MUST *NEFFER* BE USED TO HELP BRUTOPIA BEHAVE BADLY!

IT *WON'T!*

UNCLE LUDWIG GAVE ME A JACKET WITH A POCKETFUL OF *ELECTRONIC DOODADS* INSIDE! HERE'S ONE NOW!

HE SAID YOU'D KNOW WHAT TO *BUILD* WITH THESE!

⸫HMM!⸫

TASTY *BONBONS!* EAT UP!

?!

BUT DON'T WORRY!... ⸫CHOMP! CHOMP!⸫ DER *LOOK* OF DER CANDIES HAS REMINDED ME -- I HAFF A SIMILAR ITEM IN MY COAT, UND *IT* ISS ELECTRONIC!

AN *ESCAPE DEVICE* DOT LETS US *TELEPORT THROUGH WALLS...*

...BUT WE MOOST ASSEMBLE IT WITH *GREAT CARE!* ONE FALSE MOVE, UND IT CAN EXPLODE!

UNCLE LUDWIG'S FACE MUST BE RED! I BET HE HAD THE *REAL* ELECTRONIC DOODADS IN A *DIFFERENT* JACKET!

EGAD! I *SWORE* I GAVE YOUR KIDDIE A *BONBON,* MRS. HOGG!

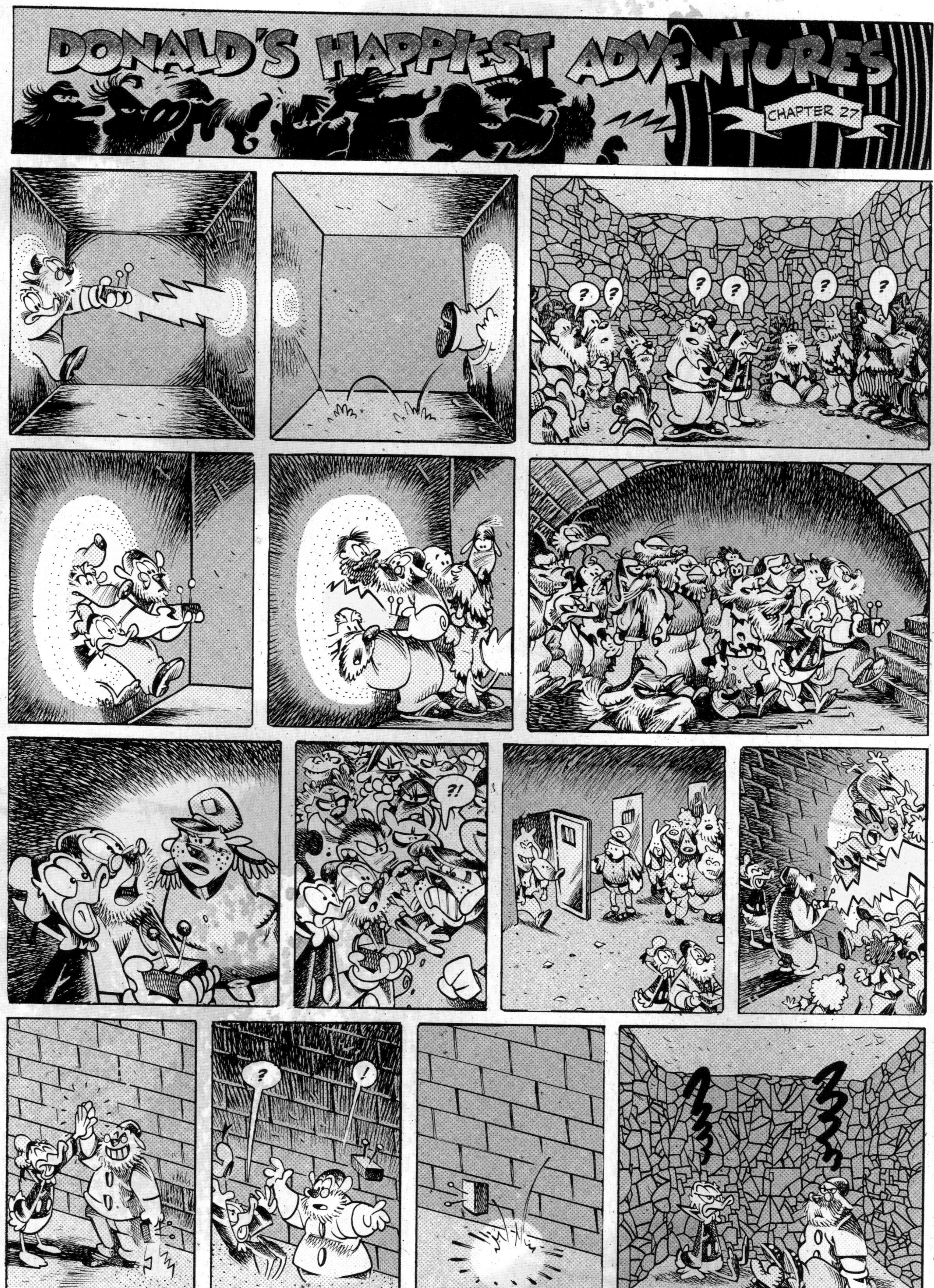
DONALD'S HAPPIEST ADVENTURES
CHAPTER 27
?
?
?
?
?
?
?!
?
!

SO *THIS* ISS HOW YOU SEEK DER SECRET OF HAPPINESS?

I THINK I'M GETTING CLOSER TO THE SECRET OF *BAD LUCK!*

-:HEH!:- THERE ISS A FAMOUS QUOTE BY AN OLD FRENCH POET...

"YOU CAN TELL HAPPINESS BY DER SOUND IT MAKES SLAMMING DER DOOR!"

WHAT THE HECK DOES *THAT* MEAN?

.DOT USUALLY, WE DO NOT *REALIZE* WHEN WE *ARE* HAPPY...

...BUT WHEN HAPPINESS *LEAVES*, WE REALIZE WE *WERE* HAPPY.

FOR EXAMPLE -- JOOST NOW, WHEN WE WERE ESCAPING -- DOT WAS A REAL SENSATION OF HAPPINESS!

BUT IT WAS *FLEETING...*

...UND WE DID NOT KNOW, AT DOT INSTANT, TO ENJOY IT WHILE WE HAD IT!

SOMETIMES WE MUST LEARN TO SAVOR DER MOMENT!

? CLICK

CLACK !

WELL? WHAT ARE *YOU* BOYS STILL DOING LOCKED UP?

BRUTOPIA'S TYRANT RULER HAS BEEN OVERTHROWN -- ALL HIS PRISONERS RELEASED!

OH, BROTHER! I'M GONNA SAVOR *THIS* MOMENT BY WALKING OUT OF PRISON *SUPER-SLOWLY!*

ME, TOO!

DING DING

DONG

AS YOU WISH... BUT THE ARMY IS MASSING TO SURROUND THE PRISON AND BREAK THE TYRANT FREE!

YOICKS! I MOVE WE FIND SUPER-SLOW HAPPINESS *TOMORROW!*

I VERY MUCH AGREE!

AS A NEW DELEGATE OF BRUTOPIA'S PROVISIONAL GOVERNMENT, I ASSURE YOU IT IS AN *HONOR* TO ACCOMPANY YOU BY PLANE!

THANKS.

NICE OF YOU.

GOOTNESS, DONALD... YOU DON'T SEEM VERY *HAPPY* TO BE GOING HOME.

BECAUSE I'M STILL STUCK *SEEKING* THE *SECRET OF HAPPINESS* FOR UNCLE SCROOGE!

->HM!<- YOU NEED TO FIND DER *STONE OF ATARAXIA.*

?

IT ISS A VERY SPECIAL ROCK DOT REMOVES ALL TROUBLES OF DER MIND!

WITH IT YOU FEEL *SOOTHED...*

YOUR MIND IN A STATE UFF IMMENSE FULLNESS!

SOUNDS LIKE A MUST-HAVE! WHERE *IS* THIS SO-CALLED STONE?

HIGH IN DER HIMALAYAS!

WOULD YOU LIKE ME TO DROP YOU OFF, MR. DUCK?

HERE WE ARE!

BUT WHERE'S THE *STONE?*

THERE... IN DER PALACE ON TOP OF DOT PEAK!

AND WHERE'S THE *AIRPORT?*

300 MILES SOUTH!

BUT I *HAPPILY* OFFER THIS *PARACHUTE.*

?!

SO? ARE YOU HAPPY THAT YOU'LL FIND HAPPINESS SOON?

HEY! YOU'RE NOT JUST TRYING TO *GET RID* OF ME, HUH? 'CAUSE YOU'VE ONLY GOT *TWO* IN-FLIGHT MEALS ABOARD?

NOT *FULL* MEALS. ONLY *PRETZEL PACKS...*

35

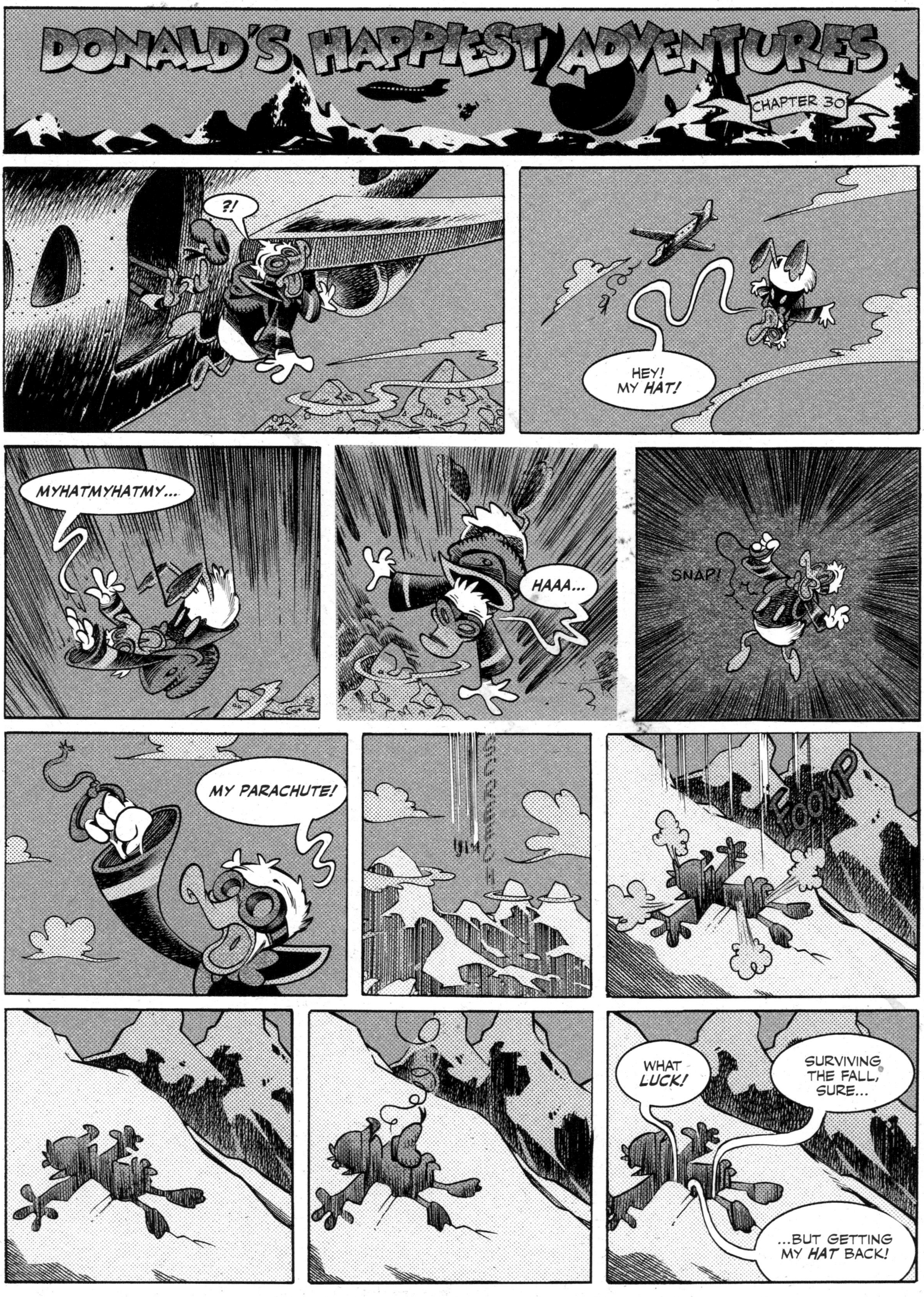
DONALD'S HAPPIEST ADVENTURES
CHAPTER 30
?!
HEY! MY HAT!
MYHATMYHATMY...
HAAA...
SNAP!
MY PARACHUTE!
FOOMP
WHAT LUCK!
SURVIVING THE FALL, SURE...
...BUT GETTING MY HAT BACK!

AND THERE'S THAT PALACE DR. EINMUG WAS BLABBING ABOUT! WOW!

ME FOR THE *STONE OF ATARAXIA!*

WAKKETY WAK!

WAIT A MINUTE! I DON'T *HAVE* THAT HAPPINESS-MAKING ROCK YET... BUT I'M *ALREADY* HAPPY!

I GUESS THAT MEANS IT'S JUST ALL THE MORE EFFECTIVE!

DIG THESE FOLKS LYING AROUND, *MEDITATING* WITH THEIR *BLISSFUL* GRINS!

THIS STONE HAS *NEXT-LEVEL* POWER!

MY HEART LEAPS UP WHEN I BEHOLD--

PEGLEG PETE!

SO WHUT, *DUCKO?* YUH WANNA *STOP* ME FROM *STEALIN'* TH' STONE OF CATARACT-WHATEVER? *BLAST* YER HIDE!

UH... PETE? YOU'RE IN SUCH AN *UGLY MOOD!* BUT THE STONE'S RIGHT *WITH* YOU IN THAT CHEST... *HOW* CAN YOU BE *MAD?* WHY AREN'T YOU *HAPPY?*

I'M HAPPY WHEN I'M MAD.

DONALD'S HAPPIEST ADVENTURES

CHAPTER 32

THANKS FOR STALLING HIM, DONALD! I'LL TAKE IT FROM HERE!

MICKEY MOUSE!

?!

HAND OVER THAT STONE OR GET *CLOBBERED!*

AN' HOW'RE YUH GONNA DO *DAT,* RUNT?

JUMP AS *HIGH* AS YUH CAN, AN' PUNCH ME IN TH' *KNEE?* →HAW! HAW!←

NOPE! BETTER!

OOH, A KICK IN TH' *DOORFRAME!*

I'M SO SCARED!

BOOM!

FAITH AN' BEJABBERS! HERE'S YOUR *CASH REWARD* FOR HELPING US CATCH PETE *AGAIN!*

THANKS, LAD!

AND TH' *GUARDIAN* OF THE ATARAXIA STONE WANTS TO THANK YA *TOO,* OL' PAL!

A *THOUSAND* THANKS!

HEY! CAN I *BUY* THAT MAGIC ROCK FROM YOU?

UH... IT'S NOT FOR SALE.

BUT IT'S NOT *MAGIC,* EITHER. IT'S JUST A *SYMBOL.*

OH, C'MON. IT CREATES HAPPINESS ALL AROUND ITSELF... DOESN'T IT?

NO, NO... NOT AT ALL!

PEOPLE HIKE FOR NINE WEEKS FROM THE OCEAN TO THIS SPOT...

...AND ALONG THE WAY, THEY DISCOVER THE WORLD'S BEAUTY! *THAT* IS WHAT MAKES THEM HAPPY!

BAH! I CAME HERE FOR *NOTHING.*

NO, YOU DIDN'T! YOUR SAILOR SUIT IS *CRAZY,* MAN! IT'S *FUNNY!* IT'S BRINGING *US HAPPINESS!*

DONALD'S HAPPIEST ADVENTURES

THERE, THERE, MY GOOD MAN. WHY ALL THIS SADNESS?

I CAN'T FIND THE SECRET OF HAPPINESS.

PERHAPS THE MORE YOU *LOOK* FOR HAPPINESS, THE LESS OF IT YOU *FIND?*

PERHAPS HAPPINESS LIES SOMEPLACE *BETWEEN* THE HARDSHIP OF WANT AND THE BOREDOM OF CONTENT!

I DON'T GET IT.

OR PERHAPS YOU SHOULDN'T TRY TO FIND HAPPINESS THROUGH PHYSICAL POSSESSIONS!

I *REALLY* DON'T GET IT.

STOP TALKING RIDDLES, MYSTERY MAN!

PERHAPS THIS, *PERHAPS* THAT...

MAKE UP YOUR *MIND!* ⇨GROWF!⇦

PERHAPS YOU SHOULD OPEN *YOUR* MIND, BOY! CHANGE THE WAY YOU LOOK AT LIFE!

IF I DO, WILL YOU STOP PERHAPSING ALREADY? ⇨WAAAK!⇦

IF YOU SAY *PERHAPS* I OUGHTTA HOLD MY TEMPER, *PERHAPS* I'LL MAKE YOU EAT ALL THE SNOW ON THIS MOUNTAIN.

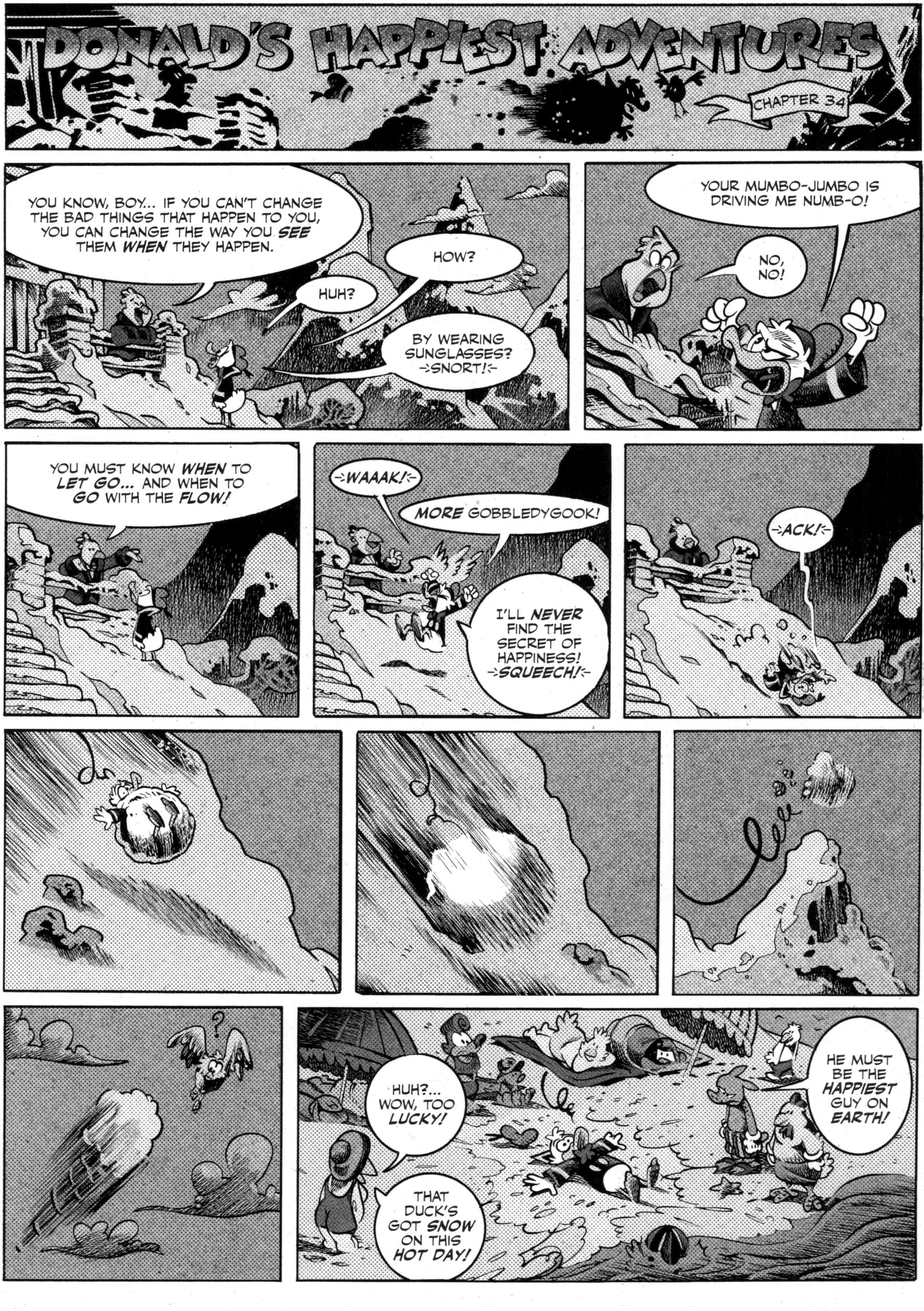

DONALD'S HAPPIEST ADVENTURES
CHAPTER 34
YOU KNOW, BOY... IF YOU CAN'T CHANGE THE BAD THINGS THAT HAPPEN TO YOU, YOU CAN CHANGE THE WAY YOU SEE THEM WHEN THEY HAPPEN.
HUH?
HOW?
BY WEARING SUNGLASSES? -SNORT!-
NO, NO!
YOUR MUMBO-JUMBO IS DRIVING ME NUMB-O!
YOU MUST KNOW WHEN TO LET GO... AND WHEN TO GO WITH THE FLOW!
-WAAAK!-
MORE GOBBLEDYGOOK!
I'LL NEVER FIND THE SECRET OF HAPPINESS! -SQUEECH!-
-ACK!-
HUH?... WOW, TOO LUCKY!
THAT DUCK'S GOT SNOW ON THIS HOT DAY!
HE MUST BE THE HAPPIEST GUY ON EARTH!

BOO-HOO-HOO!

?

WHAT'S THE MATTER, SQUIRT? YOUR MOM LOSE YOU ON THIS BEACH, OR SOMETHING?

NO-OO! ->SNIF!<-

IT'S MY CASTLE!

HOW SO?

THAT'S A CLASSY CASTLE!

NOOO-OOOO!

ER... YES! IT'S MEGA-COOL!

HIS IS BETTER! ->BWAAH!<-

->GRUMPH!<- IMAGINE THAT SCHMOE HAD NEVER BUILT HIS CASTLE! WOULDN'T YOU BE SUPER-HAPPY WITH YOUR CASTLE THEN?

MAYBE!

SEE? SO DON'T COMPARE. OTHERWISE YOU'LL ALWAYS FIND SOMETHING FLASHIER!

OOH! NICE SAILOR SUIT!

THANKS.

NO, HIS.

WOW! THAT GUY'S A REAL SAILOR!

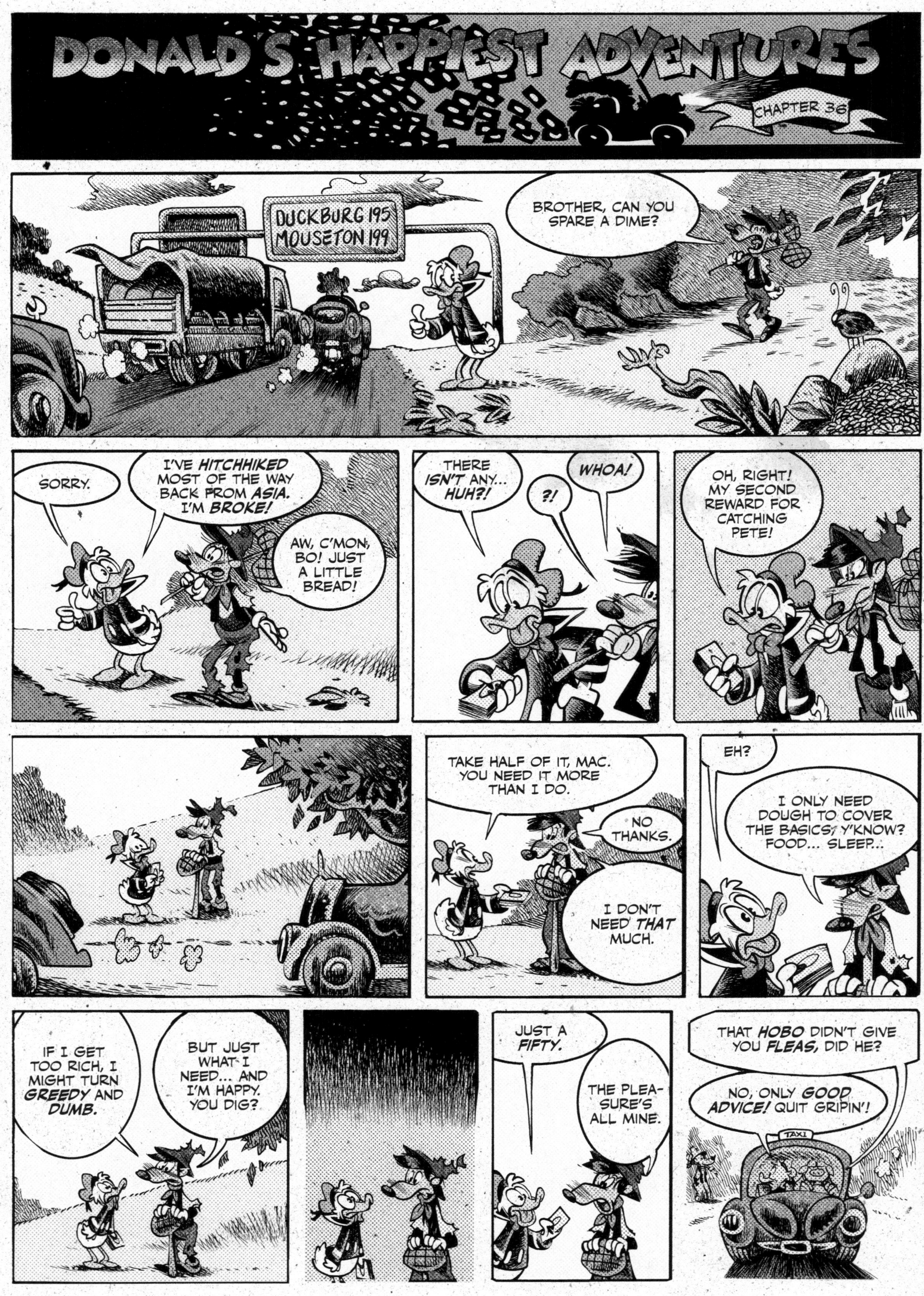
DONALD'S HAPPIEST ADVENTURES
CHAPTER 36
DUCKBURG 195
MOUSETON 199
BROTHER, CAN YOU SPARE A DIME?
SORRY.
I'VE HITCHHIKED MOST OF THE WAY BACK FROM ASIA. I'M BROKE!
AW, C'MON, BO! JUST A LITTLE BREAD!
THERE ISN'T ANY... HUH?!
?!
WHOA!
OH, RIGHT! MY SECOND REWARD FOR CATCHING PETE!
TAKE HALF OF IT, MAC. YOU NEED IT MORE THAN I DO.
NO THANKS.
I DON'T NEED THAT MUCH.
EH?
I ONLY NEED DOUGH TO COVER THE BASICS, Y'KNOW? FOOD... SLEEP...
IF I GET TOO RICH, I MIGHT TURN GREEDY AND DUMB.
BUT JUST WHAT I NEED... AND I'M HAPPY. YOU DIG?
JUST A FIFTY.
THE PLEA-SURE'S ALL MINE.
THAT HOBO DIDN'T GIVE YOU FLEAS, DID HE?
NO, ONLY GOOD ADVICE! QUIT GRIPIN'!
TAXI

-AWP!-

BOOM

WOOP! PARDON!

?!

YOU!

DONALD DUCK! MY PAL!

EH?

HEY! THE BRUTOPIAN REFUGEE!

SO! ENJOYING FREEDOM, PAL?

...YEAH, YEAH...

HOLD THE PHONE. YOU'RE NOT THRILLED?

KINDA-SORTA?

I FOUND AN APARTMENT, BUT IT'S TOO SMALL.

I STILL CAN'T WORK A MICROWAVE OVEN.

MY NEW JOB DOESN'T COME WITH ONE-YEAR VACATIONS.

AND I'VE GOTTA BUY A RECLINER FOR TV WATCHING... BUT I HAVEN'T.

ARE YOU SURE YOU WEREN'T BETTER OFF IN BRUTOPIA?

NO... ANYTHING BUT THAT!

HERE I'VE GOT AN INCREDIBLE JUICER.

THOUGH I SAW ANOTHER BRAND THAT LOOKS EVEN BETTER!

HIYA, COUSIN! WHAT'S BUZZIN'?

Fwonk Fwonk!

WELL, I--

I MET SUPERSTAR *MOLLY RINGNECK,* HERE, ON MY LAST CRUISE! NOW SHE WANTS TO SEE EVERY *INCH* OF DUCKBURG.

YOU'VE GOTTA *CHAUFFEUR* HER ALL OVER THE *CITY?* AND YOU'RE *HAPPY?*

WELL, I *WOULDN'T* BE HAPPY IF I COULDN'T *FLAUNT* MY FAMOUS FRIEND, RIGHT?

BUT WAIT...

HOLD THE PHONE, CUZ! ARE YOU *TESTING* ME? ARE YOU SAYING I CAN'T *REALLY* BE HAPPY, OR I WOULDN'T *NEED* TO SHOW OFF?

NO! NO!

I'M SAYING *DAISY* JUST WALKED OUT OF THAT SPORTS STORE UP THE BLOCK, AND SHE'S NOT THRILLED TO SEE YOU WITH YOUR... UH, FAMOUS FRIEND!

COME, DONALD. LET'S GET AWAY FROM THIS RABBLE...

...AND FIND A NICE WOODLAND GLADE FOR A *PICNIC.*

Y-YOU SURE YOU DON'T WANT TO TAKE BACK THAT TENNIS RACKET... JUST IN CASE WE'RE ATTACKED BY A HORDE OF GRIZZLIES?

CHAPTER 39

THERE'S A PERFECT SPOT BY THIS WATERFALL!

I GUESS THE FATES JUST WANT US TO PICNIC TOGETHER!

IF Y' BROUGHT THOSE VEGGIE-BURGERS LIKE LAST TIME, I'LL SWAP YOU A FIZZY POP FOR ONE!

SAY, MOUSE... I'VE GOT A QUESTION.

HOW DOES PEGLEG PETE MANAGE TO ESCAPE EVERY TIME WE CATCH HIM?

TH' DAY I CAN ANSWER THAT ONE, DONALD, I'LL GO ON A TV QUIZ SHOW AND EARN A THOUSAND BUCKS JUST LIKE NOTHIN'!

꞊GRR!꞊ CAP'S STUCK! OPEN UP, YA BIG...

PREPARE TA GET SQUISHED, SWABS!

THANKS FOR CATCHING PETE AGAIN, LADS! HERE'S YOUR CASH REWARD... AND THIS TIME, PETE, I'LL MAKE SURE DETECTIVE CASEY LOCKS YER CELL DOOR!

SO, KIDDO! WHAT GREAT TRUTHS DID YOU FINALLY LEARN?

THAT UNCLE SCROOGE IS GONNA TWIST MY HEAD OFF!

HO, HO! HE COULDN'T DO *THAT!* IT WOULD REQUIRE MUSCLE MASS OF $3G + \dfrac{SM}{U}$...

OH!

BUT I NEVER *DID* FIND HIM THE SECRET OF HAPPINESS!

HE'LL BE RAVING FURIOUS!

...NOW, TO TWIST OFF YOUR *LEGS* HE'D NEED *JUST* AS MUCH STRENGTH AS FOR YOUR HEAD.

YOUR *ARMS* ARE A *LITTLE* WEAKER!

BUT YOU DON'T GOTTA BE *TOO* SCARED...

IT WAS JUST A FIGURE OF SPEECH.

~HMM!~

...UNLESS HE USES A *LEVER!*

HE *WON'T!* LOOK, I'M GOOD, OKAY?

OR A FORKLIFT! OR A CRANE...

OR EVEN A STEAM SHOVEL!

I. AM. FINE.

...OR IF HE CONNECTED A LEVER TO A CLAMP...

GREAT. I'M *GOING* NOW.

HOW MUCH WORSE CAN UNCLE LUDWIG MAKE A BAD IDEA? THE WORLD MAY NEVER KNOW!

"DEAR UNCLE SCROOGE..."

"TO ACHIEVE HAPPINESS, YOU *MUST*..."

...GO TAKE A HIKE?

...GIVE MORE THAN YOU RECEIVE?

...KNOW YOUR INNER DUCK?

:...GAG YOUR GREED!

...BE CONTENT WITH YOUR LOT!

...QUIT GETTING STEAMED ABOUT THINGS YOU CAN'T CONTROL!... NAH! HE COULD *NEVER*!...

AH!

DONALD!

WELL?

DID YOU FIND THAT *AZTEC TREASURE TEMPLE* LIKE I ASKED?

ER...

I...

HUH?

NOPE. DIDN'T FIND IT, UNK.

SORRY. *REALLY.*

BUT GOOD NEWS! YOU DON'T NEED TO REIMBURSE ME FOR THE COSTS OF THE TRIP!

HEY, I GAVE HIM HAPPINESS, DIDN'T I?

I *COULDA* DEMANDED PAY!

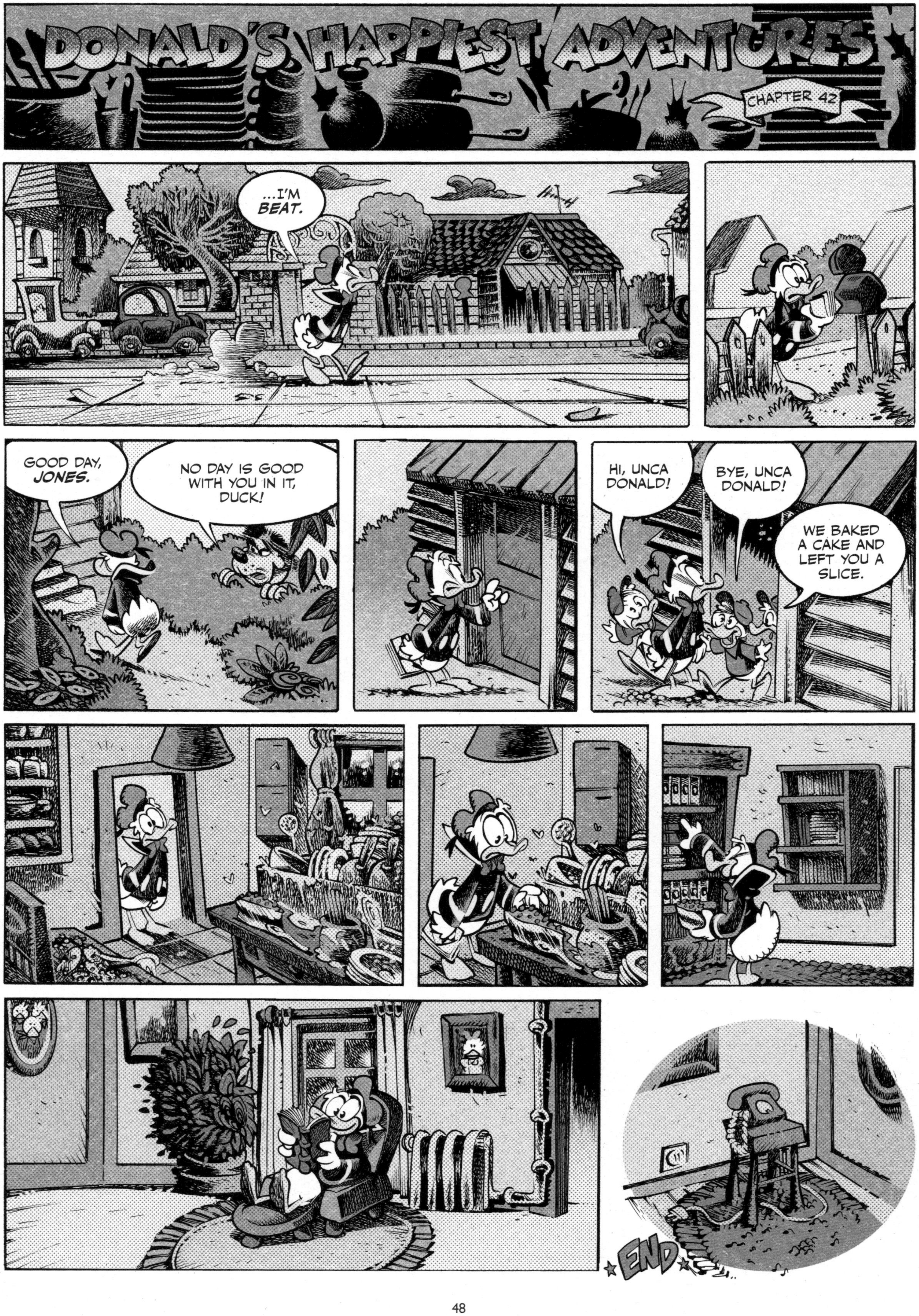
DONALD'S HAPPIEST ADVENTURES
CHAPTER 42
...I'M BEAT.
GOOD DAY, JONES.
NO DAY IS GOOD WITH YOU IN IT, DUCK!
HI, UNCA DONALD!
BYE, UNCA DONALD!
WE BAKED A CAKE AND LEFT YOU A SLICE.
END

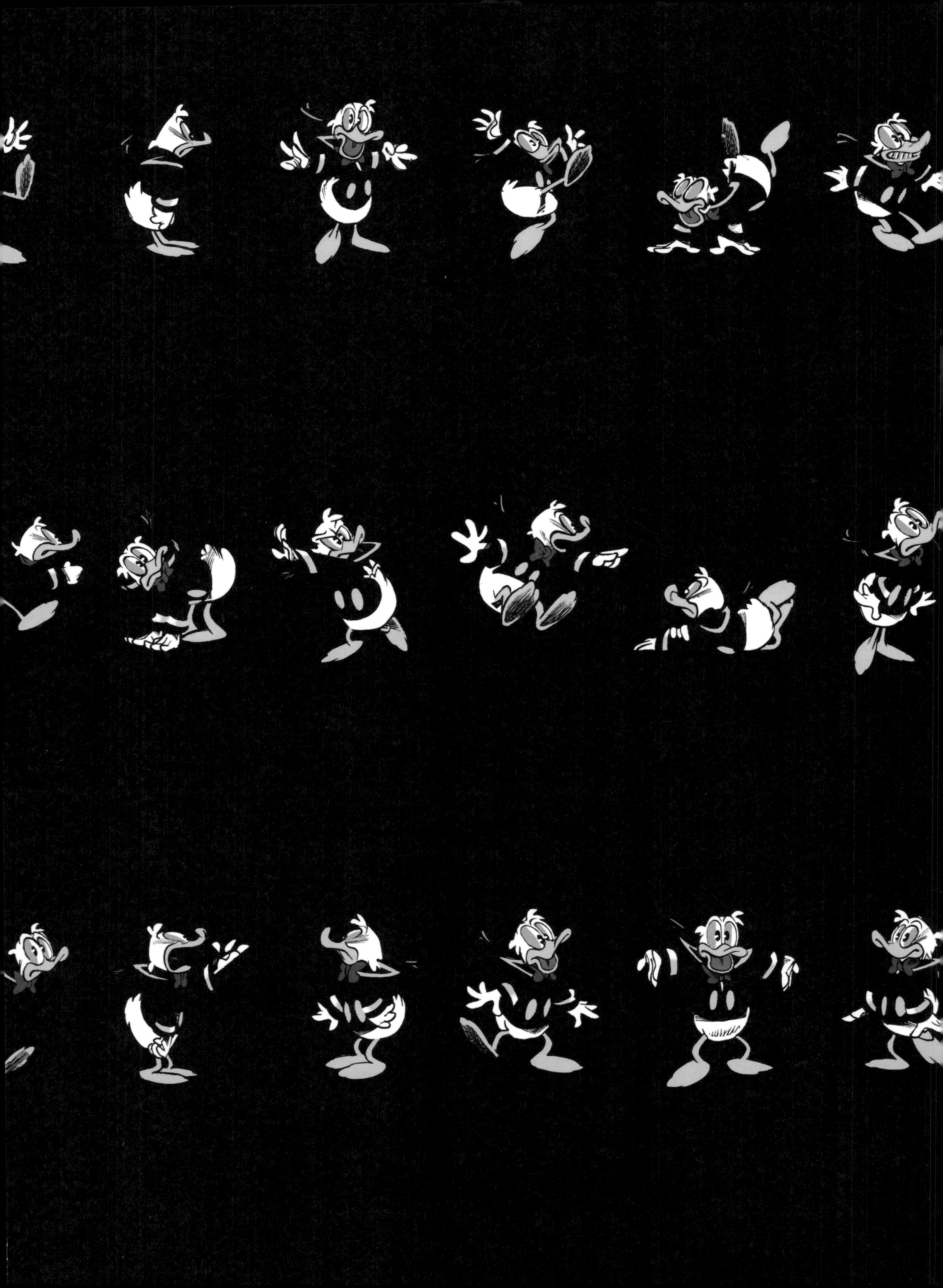